Thoughts Of a Depressed Human

# Table of Contents

## Generations

Same anecdotes,

Different narratives.

You've grown muted in your old age.

You have suddenly decided to care.

And I'm regretful to hear that.

I used to look up to you,

And now I wish you didn't exist.

You see her as a delicate dinner plate,

That you only get out for special occasions.

You are mortified of me,

Of what I became.

Just because I don't look like the image in your head,

Doesn't mean I'm broken.

You apologise but I could never take you seriously.

Where was my special treatment?

She's receiving everything I needed.

Because I wasn't abnormal enough for your interest.

I've never seen you shed a tear; that frightened me.

I understand it now.

We are meant to be silent; we are meant to be content.

She screamed loud enough,

She didn't listen to you shouting over and over to grow up. I did.

# Love Robot

Love is a chemical; even emotionless people can desire something.

I see people as objects,

If they gratify me, make me happy enough that I don't want to leave.

Then I won't; I don't.

However, infuriate me enough and I will disappear.

You do not have the gift to keep me.

I am as cold as ice; as hard as nails.

But when I am with you that dissolves away.

Why?

I shout as I shake your helpless body.

You have spiked my drinks for life and I cannot stay away.

You say you love me; I see you say the same words as you end the phone call with her.

You say you miss me; you never see me.

You tell me to wait; I am impatient.

You say all the right words, yet your actions mean nothing.

You get angry when I do not believe you,

But what do you expect?

I don't like being treated like a stray dog.

I don't like you assuming I will follow you around because I have nothing else.

Love is just a chemical.

Like a light switch; I can turn it off.

But every time you shove, I allow it.

Every time you fuck up, I'm the one apologising.

Every time a scar appears on my left arm, I take responsibility.

It is all my fault.

I lie there on the floor,

And wonder why people walk all over me.

"You used to critique my nudes like they were fucking art work. I'm sorry I wasn't art to you"

## Promises

He promises never to leave me.

He promises to stay by my side,

As long as my legs are wide.

Open.

## Opposites Attract

You were fire

And I was water

You were light

And I was darkness

Opposites attract

They just don't stay together

We tried to fix each other

And that's how you got burnt

You were sugar

I was salty

Imperfectly perfect

You were in colour

I was in black and white

You were music

I was silence

You loved me


I didn't love you at all.

# Blue-Eyed Girl

I wanted her.

She was genuine and beautiful.

And I was dishonest.

I wanted her to feel my fingerprints.

All over her perfect figure.

Over her curves.

The scars on her arms screamed at me.

But I knew I couldn't ask.

I already knew the situation.

She was broken.

I was cracked.

And we didn't have any glue.

## Apathy

I want love.    I yearn for unstable.   I need to be up at three in the morning. I  hunger  to  be  able  to  need someone.  I love objects and materials.       Because that's easy.       But I want someone to make me feel sick with love.       Nauseous  of  the  thought  of  losing  them.          I desire a purpose.    I don't want to be able to walk away from the situation.          With  barely  a  tear on my face.    I need to feel.          How  can  I  expect anyone to love me?    If I can't love them?  I want to be completely on top of the world.        As well as being so close to hell.          I  want  to  get  so  fixated  with another individual.    That I remember the exact shape of their eyes.       And the colour they glow.    I want to feel butterflies.       I want to get anxious.I  want  to  have  a reason to impress someone.  I want pain.    A         fire burning throughout my heart and veins.
          Rather   than   being   stone   cold   constantly.
          Candles rather than ice cubes. I want to feel alive.
          I want a fucking reason to feel happiness.      I want dopamine.       Instead of a zombified soul.

## My Innocent Lover

Warmth fills your eyes,

When you look at me.

Your hands against mine.

I want to forget the world with you.

Love is doing something you absolutely hate.

For someone who probably doesn't deserve it.

# Alive

Just because I survived doesn't mean I want to be a survivor.

All you witness is the strong outer layer I put up for people.

You don't suspect any tear stained cheeks.

You don't assume I'm screaming,

Pulling my hair,

Punching the walls,

Cutting my arms,

Wanting it all to stop.

Why won't it bloody stop?

If there is some white guy up there who believes he's God

Then why does he make me go through the same torture over and over again.

But you all think I'm strong.

I don't feel very strong,

Sat here,

Wishing I was dead.

Don't fall in love with me,

You'll be falling in love with a dead girl.

I'm a fraud.

Can't you see that?

I'm sorry to have led you into thinking I was something I'm not.

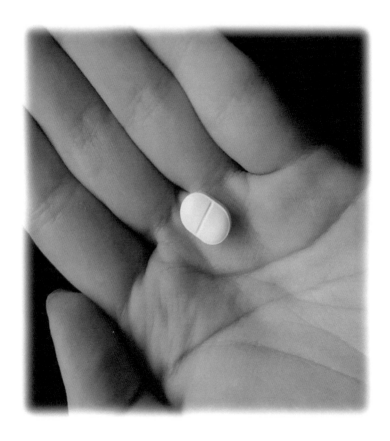

# Prescriptions

This little pill.

The little white powdered

mess in my hands.

Holds my happiness.

My shield against the world.

It's not working.

It's not fucking working.

I scream at the four walls surrounding me.

What am I meant to do now?

I'm sleeping beauty.

But with short hair.

And a desire never to wake up again.

## Almost Lover

Thank you, kind sir.

I appreciate what you have done here.

You have made me stronger,

Less naïve.

I can never find good in people anymore,

Even if it is slapping me across the face.

I'm terrified of trust.

I have this pit of repressed rage,

Sat at the bottom of my stomach,

And I'm not sure what I am meant to do with it.

I search for you in other partners.

Trying to find a reason to self-destruct.

Thanks to you,

I'm frightened of the dark,

Being alone and vulnerable.

Don't worry, I don't want you dead.

I want life to torture the living shit out of

You.

## Feeling Blue

Infant children.

Pretending to be something; imagined being superhuman.

How old do you have to be before that game doesn't work?

End of the day you still end up in bed.

As the pitiful, pathetic girl in your head.

Pretend to be happy and you eventually will be.

That's what they said.

But it isn't working.

I don't have the imagination.

To trick my mind into feeling any variation.

You tell me.

I have to be fine.

I have everything anyone could ever want,

How can that make me feel so weakened?

Nothing makes me content anymore.

Does that make me unappreciative?

I'm disorientated.

And I need you to believe that I'm not lying.

It's not something you can see, like a wound or a bruise,

But it still destroys me.

Don't ask me to explain it.

The chemicals in my brain can't work out if I deserve to be feeling this way.

I just do.

# Friends?

I miss him,

I miss the way he used to care.

The way I was the single most important person to him.

Now I'm the last on his list.,

In the back of his brain.

How the tables have turned.

I didn't need him to begin with,

And now I can't have him.

Why do I care?

It shouldn't bother me,

But it seems it does.

The ants crawling up my legs,

Seem to be giving me more attention

Than him.

I can't waste my time getting upset,

Over someone who won't get upset over me.

He probably doesn't even realise.

And I want it to stay that way.

I'm glad he's happy.

Seems I was just a temporary fix.

Till he found her.

You just fucked off.

Thanks for being everything,

You said you hated.

For everything you promised you wouldn't turn into.

He walked out on me whilst,

I was mentally slitting my wrists.

He gave me the rope

And closed the door.

It seems I am too complicated for people.

Feeling too much or not enough.

I'm not entirely sure,

What people want from me.

Part of me trusted him,

Part of me saw this coming.

And yet it still surprised me.

I didn't care.

But he made me. So god damn much.

# Rainy Days

You know you're fucked when those 1am thoughts,

Start to appear in the afternoon.

You were starting to believe what your parents said about you;

You are just an ungenerous, ungrateful child.

All you do is think about yourself.

Do something for someone else for once in your life.

And I did.

I gave him my world for I felt that was how much he was worth.

And there were moments where I think he thought the same.

But something changed within him.

He changed.

Maybe he had demons like me.

But his were narcissistic heart breakers related to the devil. Once his needs were met I was no longer necessary.

But I loved him.

I didn't care I just wanted to be with him.

Even if it meant crying my eyes out as soon as I got home.

Vodka became my best friend.

The strong kick to my throat hurt.

But not as much as him.

He told me he wouldn't hurt me. Yet he did.

He told me he wouldn't leave me.

Yet he did.

I don't want to go to sleep.
He is in my dreams

# Dear Past Lover

You are the reason I cry at night.

The reason I desire to be alone,

Drinking.

The reason I blast my ears full of depressingly true words.

I have no confidence in anything I do.

I'm scared of failing,

Disappointing.

You are the reason I can never trust a single soul again.

I let you in. into my naïve heart.

And you ripped it.

Because you could.

I can imagine you sitting, thinking, laughing about what you did.

You gave me warning signs I couldn't see.

You broke me yet I'm the one apologising.

You are the reason for the late night google searches,

On how to forget someone,

Forever.

I want to tell people but at the same time I'm ashamed of the secret.

You used me.

Abused me.

And whilst I shiver myself to sleep every evening,

You don't even remember my name.

## Noise Cancelling

They all tell me, it's going to be okay.

But I don't want it to be okay.

I want it to stop.

You stopped asking if I was
okay,
And I stopped saying no.
You already knew,
I'm sorry for making you
feel like it was,
Something you could fix.
In me.

## Naked

It's easy to get naked,

The difficult thing is to let them read your soul.

To let them into your mind.

To let them know how vulnerable you really are.

Your weaknesses, your strengths.

What keeps you up at night.

What makes you laugh.

What makes you cry.

You'll fall in love with my body time and time again.

But my brain is far less beautiful.

Please don't run away when you see my flaws.

## Depression

It's not just about feeling numb and empty.

It's not just about feeling lonely and invisible in a crowd full of people.

It's the waking up wishing you were dead.

And it's not about what all the insecure pretty girls are saying,

About sleeping forever.

It's about wishing you didn't exist.

It's about being in so much pain.

That each day drags on,

Like you're carrying a boulder everywhere you go.

## Where Does It Hurt?

Breathe.

Inhale and exhale.

It's okay for the tears to stream down your face.

It's okay for no one to see.

It's okay for everyone to see.

It's okay to not be okay.

You poor angel of a human being.

Who did this to you?

They asked you where he hurt you,

And you point to the head of the doll.

Maybe he only touched me once,

But he's fucked me for life.

## Warmth

Your deep brown eyes.

Your caramel skin.

Your warm heart.

You give me knots in my hair.

And knots in my stomach.

What can you see every time you look deep into my eyes?

I want to shake the answer out of you until you are blue in the face.

## Fear of Abandonment

Sometimes I can't sleep so I think of you.

And sometimes I think of you so much that I can't sleep.

Why do your eyes leak,

Young girl are you scared?

Scared that this is the happiest you have ever been,

And it could be torn away?

From you.

But you trust that it won't.

Maybe it isn't the horror films that scare you.

It is falling in love with someone.

And finding out they don't love you back.

## Autism

Maybe I was drawn to you because you were different,
Because I needed to find someone to understand me.
For my differences.
You seem to bring myself out of me.
The little girl that got bullied for being weird,
You would hold her hand and tell her,
It's okay.
Society is full of sheep.
But you told me it was okay to be a thunderstorm,
To be unique .
Being different doesn't make you any less,
Human.
Everyone makes mistakes,
My mistake was not letting you in sooner.
I tried so hard to be honest.
Because the world is full of enough,
Liars and cheaters.
And I don't want to be one of them.
I want to hold you,
Over and over,

Until the world stops
Turning.

## Our Future

I want to be able to look at you,

And see the future.

See the wrinkles start to form on your face,

Where you spent years laughing,

Where you spent years loving,

Me.

I may have never been your first,

But I can't wait to be your last.

I don't like the idea of growing old,

With you it doesn't seen too scary.

## Whiskey Nights In

Just because I didn't remember,

Doesn't mean I said yes.

Sometimes silence is louder than screams.

## Weather Forecast

Oh, dark cloud above my head,

Why you so grey?

I miss the sunshine,

The rainbows,

And the stars.

All I see is rain, why won't you stop raining?

I'm scared of the dark.

Of the unknown.

I'm cold.

So cold.

Oh grey cloud above my head.

Why won't you leave me be?

I can't see what is in front of me.

## Depression Naps

The grease clings to my hair,

The smell of two-day old socks,

Lingers in the air.

I'm too tired to shower,

Or to care.

What people think.

I may have made it into work,

But that's only because,

I can't stand to be at home.

Alone.

Where my thoughts are so loud.

People might hear.

Go away.

You don't deserve to see me,

Like this.

## Invisible Illness

I may not look ill,

But I am.

I am really sick.

And like any sick person,

I need support,

And care,

And love.

And someone to tell me,

It is all going to be okay.

I don't need someone calling me,

Lazy,

And selfish.

I already feel like a waste,

Of oxygen.

You don't need to make that thought.

Louder.

## Perfectionist

Life happened to me.

Bad people happened to me.

Bad things happened to me.

And I tried to fix them.

I'm a thinker.

I like to solve problems.

And puzzles.

I tried to fix you.

To change you.

I should have been.

Fixing myself.

## Love Battles

I don't know what's worse.

Loving someone who doesn't

love you back.

Or being loved by someone

you don't love.

Being broken

Or breaking a soul.

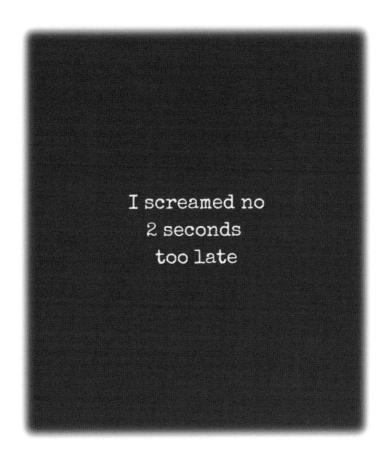

I screamed no
2 seconds
too late

## Blame Game

I lost my childhood years,

Because of you.

I lost my innocence,

Because of you.

Had to mature so much quicker,

Than I wanted to,

Because of you.

I'm a baby face,

With stressed out wrinkles,

On her forehead.

Where I was constantly pushed,

To grow up.

When I didn't want to,

Because of you.

## Torture Victim

I want to see what I wasted,

My energy on.

Did I deserve any of this?

Probably not.

Does that matter?

No.

What happened, happened.

Nothing I can do to change the past.

The thing that scares me,

The most.

Is wondering if I was the only victim

Oh, kind sir,

Were there other girls?

Because I wouldn't want,

Anyone else to take this torture on.

## Favouritism

I want to know.
If I was your only girl,
Not because I'm green,
With envy,
Because compared to what was,
Really going on,
Cheating would have been,
The best thing you could do to me,
I want to know.
If they were all getting,
The same treatment as me,
Or was I your favourite,
The only one you truly loved,
Maybe you treated me the way,
You did,
Because you were petrified,
From the truth,
I want to know.
If this was your intention,
From the start,

Or whether the situation confused you,
And you went spiralling down.

## Aidan

All the ways you make me feel,

Ignite the love I feel for you.

Day after day, I think I cannot love you,

Any more than I already do.

Never ending memories of you.

Printed in Great Britain
by Amazon

30873380R00037